I0170014

Song Poems in Search of Music

JOE FARLEY

SUNBURY PRESS

Mechanicsburg, Pennsylvania   USA

Published by Sunbury Press, Inc.
50 West Main Street, Suite A
Mechanicsburg, Pennsylvania 17055

www.sunburypress.com

For information about special discounts for bulk purchases, please contact Sunbury Press Orders Dept. at (855) 338-8359 or orders@sunburypress.com.

To request one of our authors for speaking engagements or book signings, please contact Sunbury Press Publicity Dept. at publicity@sunburypress.com.

ISBN: 978-1-62006-419-1 (Trade Paperback)

FIRST SUNBURY PRESS EDITION: May 2014

Product of the United States of America
0 1 1 2 3 5 8 13 21 34 55

Set in Garamond
Designed by Lawrence Knorr
Cover by Lawrence Knorr
Edited by Lawrence Knorr

Continue the Enlightenment!

Introduction

I've been writing poetry on and off (mostly off) for more than thirty years. In 2013, it came to me that maybe I should pursue actually publishing some of them. With that in mind, I unearthed a box long buried in the attic, to review what lay within. I liked some of the poems, and began to write more, yet again. Thus, this book contains poems written from the 1970s to the present day. This process turned out to me a far more difficult task than I thought it would be. I learned, at least for me, that poetry is very personal.

I decided on the title "Song Poems in Search of Music" because, in many cases, the poems reminded me of song lyrics. In addition, while I am a big fan of poetry, including Shakespeare's sonnets, Wordsworth, Poe and William Butler Yeats, I've been heavily influenced by the more current singer/songwriters. For those reasons, the title seemed appropriate.

The book, in some ways, became a family affair. My wife (who had to put up with my mood changes while I wrote this) provided the photos. I also included two poems that were written by my oldest son, Corrigan. I didn't leave out my other boys, Jim and Ben, as they were the inspiration for the poem titled "Twins." I really have to thank all of them, as together they bring music into my life on a daily basis.

I also want to mention the support I received from Joe Farrell (my co-author of the "Keystone Tombstones" series), as he provided me with plenty of encouragement as I worked on this project. He did so, despite the fact that it took time away from a book we were working on together. I am also appreciative of the support I received from my publisher, Lawrence Knorr at Sunbury Press, who was willing to take a chance on these poems. In addition I'd be remiss if I didn't mention the people I've met over the years that caused me to sit down and put pen to paper and actually write the verses, even though some of the poems are so old I can't remember who they were about.

It is my hope that you, the reader, find some pleasure as you go through this volume. Finally, if any of you are musicians, feel free to find the music the lines within may be searching for.

---- Joe Farley, 2014

Perfectly Pennswood

I abandoned the burdens years ago,
Things were moving too fast and I took them too slow.
I remember the day that you were unmasked.
Would you have told me the truth had I ever asked?
Now my table is set and I haven't a care,
You may be out there someplace, I just don't know where.
You might be in Europe or maybe in Dixie,
I'm thinking of taking a sip of my whiskey.

There are days I still wonder and nights I still dream,
In the latter, things are really not as they seem.
There's pain that can lock you behind bars of steel
And scars that can take a whole lifetime to heal.
But for now all is quiet—my seas remain calm,
Yesterday held the darkness, but I swear by the dawn.
I don't dwell on the past, my eyes don't get misty,
I'm thinking of taking a sip of my whiskey.

Some folks live in silence and some swim in lies,
But it's the truth when they tell you that time really flies.
People keep chirping saying "back in the day..."
I choose to ignore them. I can't live that way.
There will always be trouble—life is sometimes unfair.
I glance in the mirror. I don't stand there and stare.
I suppose we took chances and we learned that was risky,
But, for now, I'll be taking a sip of my whiskey.

It's Getting Late Early

A man stands outside smoking.
A pretty girl is on my right.
This place is dark and crowded.
It might be time to say 'goodnight.'
When a song is warm and caring,
Sometimes the evil princess dances.
There are some roads too hard to travel,
And there are days you take your chances.
I'm looking at the calendar, but I can't make out the date.
It's really way too early to get the feeling it's this late.

There are stories out there somewhere
That can cling and tie you tight.
I'm still hard at work on something,
But it never turns out right.
Across the street a bridge is burning.
The silence grows to thunder in my head.
I've been down that way before
And learned that's not a path to tread.
You may not be a sinner, but god knows you're not a saint.
It's really way too early to get the feeling it's this late.

Some dark clouds are slow in moving.
It takes years for them to pass.
There are days that we all struggle
As we try to dodge the lash.
The icy wind is blowing.
There are times you miss the feast.
It's true that you can reach the point
Where you can't tell the beauty from the beast.
The fisherman sits patiently, dangling the bait.
It's really way too early to get the feeling it's this late.

The Promise

In those hours between the darkness, dimmed to daylight,
When the forces of desire start to grow,
On my own, but in the long run, feeling alright,
Though that's balanced by all the things I've come to know.
I learned this is a world of planned confusion,
Where one wanders in a web of broken glass.
Breaking free, you look at life and its illusions,
Watching comics, ever so tragically, pass.
Although that's so and the memory is a creature,
Who lacks the teeth to test the truths of time,
All in all, that is it's most attractive feature—
Allowing welcomed rest to weary minds.

I'm well aware the danger posed by the hearts exposure.
More than once I found it knocked me to the floor.
But in the end, we always build such weak enclosures
And rush to answer all our unlatched doors.
In those moments when you face your life's disruptions,
In those minutes that strain before they pass,
I swear you feel an inner strength's eruption,
When, upon the rock of fire, your hopes are dashed.
There are dreams that have to wait until tomorrow.
There are winds that seem to hum a melody.
To be honest, there is little need for sorrow.
Lift up your head and find the remedy.

In faint recall, I still can glimpse a meeting,
Too calm to lay beyond mystery's glance,
But, to this day, I wonder what provoked the greeting
And, worse, what made them want to take a chance?
The faster that I rush, I'm less in motion.
There's no desert rain—no scratches in the sand.
Today, no longer strangled by emotion,
I can understand what sense to understand.
But, the saddest tale of all on which I've spoken,
Beyond the horizon, I watch as shadows fall,
Upon the promise laying out there broken,
Until I can't remember her at all.

A Tinge of Philosophy

Of use, the herd, a place to hide,
Forfeiting life amusingly,
In a carnival of circus wheels
Rolled by clowns of misery.
I have seen it doesn't faze you—
Watched you wipe the dust away—
The clearest glass, the smell of time,
As the hands tick off the day.
There is a call that waits for each a turn—
Is but a shriek this banshee's cry.
Each path, at end, she calls her own.
Makes little sense, this quest for why.
Could the wisest one among us
Explain a simple truth?
Watch as he evades the question,
While he waves a flag of truce.
So dwell little on the why of things,
Or on the way there apt to be—
Just move from one day to the next.
That is your eternity.

Circles and Squares

In the back of my mind, I knew it was my turn.
I always admitted I had plenty to learn.
You took it with you, though it was nothing you earned.
I kept my eyes on the bridges, watching them burn.
There is noise in the attic—footsteps on the stairs.
There's a man on the TV talking foreign affairs.
The mistake took a minute. I abandoned all cares.
You had the circles. I had the squares.

The winter's upon us. You need to trek through the snow.
You had reason to leave, but nowhere to go.
I suppose that it's true; you have to reap what you sow.
I was thinking of all the things you'll never know.
You can't tell my age from the grey of my hair.
You had little to give and even less you would share.
You refuse to admit it and that's simply unfair.
You had the circles. I had the squares.

I never did well on horseback; that wasn't my style.
There's plenty of time. I think I'll rest for awhile.
I have nothing to hide. You can check out my file.
That road was a long one; it stretched on for miles.
Some things are too heavy—not a weight I can bear.
You don't say a word; you just stand there and stare.
I hate to admit it, but we made quite the pair.
You had the circles. I had the squares.

A Fool's Heart

It was past midnight when I confessed,
My comedic days lived as a clown,
Whose every breath became burlesque,
Whose very breath was almost drowned
In the strained abstraction of suspense,
And the strange delights of those days downed.

Thus I had explained my fate.
She advised luxuriate.

Within the beating of a fool's heart,
I mistook lust for so much more.
And as my youth was ripped apart,
By screams or by the whispered word,
The guilt that I felt for my part
Fled upon the wings of birds.

I felt the heat of hate abate.
She advised luxuriate.

Was thus we waited dusk to dawn—
A dawn that would come all too soon.
For once the dark of night was drawn
Into the hum of mornings tune,
I thought about all I'd been shown
Beneath that marvelous harvest moon.

There was so much left to contemplate.
She advised luxuriate.

We lay awake and share in thought
All that we still dare to think.
I face a find far too long sought
In the emptied glass of too much drink.
A soul freed of the if and but,
No longer standing on the brink.

I suggested that we celebrate.
She advised luxuriate.

Lines Composed on November 26, 1982 (Thoughts of Glass)

I whispered softly to the ghost,
And watched her fade away,
As each word drifted aimlessly
Into the darkness of decay.
The shadows of the night loomed large.
The moon was swallowed whole.
The mist of sadness reached my heart,
And it blew around my soul.
Thoughts of glass—thoughts of stone;
I knew you'd never make it on your own!
A broken heart will heal in time,
Just like a broken bone.

She took a coin into her hand;
I watched her fingers fold.
That iron grip proclaimed to all
Her high regard for gold.
Months later, when the sun grew hot,
The truth came in my sleep.
A child with parents such as these,
Would have just cause to weep.
Thoughts of glass—thoughts of stone;
I know you never liked to be alone!
A broken heart will heal with time,
Just like a broken bone.

The reflection of the year gone past
Strikes me like a joke.
I watched you stare for hours on end,
Until the mirror broke.
One would think that you'd have learned by now,
Though it's plain that you can't tell.
Love is something that you make;
Not something that you sell.
Thoughts of glass—thoughts of stone;
Someday we'll all be wearing telephones!
A broken heart will heal with time,
Just like a broken bone.

On Meeting Eros

I can sense she's in the foyer; the scent of sweet bouquet
Rises up to greet me through the walls.
But, it's a walk on broken glass
And one stumbles as one fumbles,
With affection's mask, until it falls.
Then all shields removed, defenses down,
A naked rider through the fog;
Where she alone has any will to see
Beyond the tug of beauty, that magnet of slow melt,
That offers freedom sacrificially.
But I could liberate that legend,
And face the many sided door;
Ignore the force of fears run through my veins.
In the window of the future
Hurl the sorrows of the past.
Let feeling creep from under years of strain.
She lands softly beside me,
A fall in round dark almond eyes.
As she turns, she hears the scream of storms neglect.
She looks at me; I burn.
Without words she speaks. I learn
That I have no idea what's coming next.

On the Lost Legends

Surrounded by these waters, ripples' edge reaching,
Rocks sunk forgotten, thrown too long ago.
The sun-pierced mist a lightened veil
Covering, in mock concealment, scenes the past may know.
Shyly she moves to be moved,
Mocking the age old question, dream or real?
Even if we had the answer, what would be proved?
That which has been said or the way it makes us feel.
Though one is one to compute camouflages the cost,
For every legend that lives, another legend's been lost.

So much magic has disappeared, and amusement.
It was shared by many, though too few at the time.
Some fools demand that the game be played on the circle's edge.
But, bronze or stone, what rule stands up in rhyme?
Enchanted, pursued, pushed by pride,
The joking of more than thirty years now asked for a measure;
The boy may be aging and he has nowhere to hide;
Perhaps on the tower, where a king counts his treasure.
With that very thought comes a wind ripe with frost.
For every legend that lives, another legend's been lost.

The clock ticking, who knows what arrows wait to strike.
Questions spark answers that beg to be mocked.
The cycle, this cycle, both absurd and arrogant,
Locked the very moment that it's unlocked.
Such thoughts, thinking, naked consumption undraped;
In youth, passion in manhood never spent.
Why so forgetful? You know how the words escaped.
You are both prey and predator, as one invents.
Alone await tomorrow, somewhat seasoned, somewhat tossed,
For every legend that lives, another legend's been lost.

Insight

Sleeping soundly—or thought he was—
When she blew through his brain.
He asked her, "Why?" She said, "Because."
Then they got on the train.
A passing porter grabbed her arm,
While pushing him away.
He hit, by chance, the train's alarm,
Which forced them all to stay.
But broken trains must move along,
And each one does somehow.
He watched it wondering what went wrong,
Never knowing until now.

The Cat on the Windowsill

Though this late hour finds me midnight weary,
On the birthday eve of the gentle lady, I remain wary
Not to speak too loud for poetry.
Should, like a breeze, search silently,
Through the hour or through the day,
To find expressions that so convey,
The secret, yet keep secrets still,
As a cat leaps atop the windowsill.

Twenty years and eight, still there are decades that must die
Before the days celebration appears in an old mother's eye.
And within the sight that scans those years,
She recalls a life in another hemisphere.
It appears our meeting was too calm by chance
To lie outside mere circumstance.
But as time passes, we will wait until
The cat leaps atop the windowsill.

She, in her laughter, told me just yesterday
That I was mistaking brown hair for grey.
And I felt that dancing deep in my heart,
Not unlike that first evening when, a table apart,
I held in my thought, thoughts for none but her ears
Of a high handed love—a love not made for those years.
When she touched my hand, all that was moving grew still
Save for the cat leaping from the windowsill.

The Dark-Eyed Girl

My mind's on fire and no one's unconcerned while burning.
The dark-eyed girl, she takes it for a ride.
And me, a mere word player in a windstorm,
What words to deal once candor's been defied?
At best, well, my beginnings sure were humble.
At worst, I had those days when pain would pound.
The dark-eyed girl has secrets that she tells me
To close the heart and seal the soul with sound.
No limit to this limbo, so I raise torches
Above a mist that all but leaves you blind.
The dark-eyed girl equates each turn with pleasure,
And, me, well I guess all good roads must wind.
There's a thunder that I hear when her lips quiver.
I'm in a parade that circles round the clock.
The dark-eyed girl stands tall, not ever bending
Down to touch the key left in my lock.
The dagger of the deed is used and bloody,
Laid sliced before me all I thought was true.
The window's caked with mud; the house abandoned,
And dark-eyed girls that look a lot like you.
The mirror spits each image that it reflects.
The dark-eyed girl's been standing there too long,
And I'm not ever sad, not ever dreaming.
It's hard to tell which one of us is wrong.
Door handles, broken glasses, a dark-eyed girl, this farce;
Of tempers tames just in the nick of time.
You say the loss of stem and root has left you destitute
As you confess, that does not meet up to mind.

I Should Have Been A Congressman

I should have been a Congressman.
I have corruption in my veins.
A silly smile, an itchy palm,
I see money when it rains.
And though I'm not a Congressman,
I do not hold a grudge.
For in addition to the robes,
I stay sober as a judge.
Now give me a second to count all this bounty.
As you may have guessed, I'm from Luzerne County.

Lines Composed in the Bottle
(The Goat Song)

Of course there was that chance meeting,
One evening of classical mimicry;
Born breathless like so many ideas casting shadows even in the
shade, unfortunately.
We passed in a bar with a nod,
Sober, so manners held sway over feelings.
The cowboy ordered a couple beers,
As you two proceeded to discuss double-dealing.
At midnight, confronted by the kidnapper of truth,
Time, within its claws, all with any worth, is torn.
Do you really believe it was any different then,
When dust next to nothing was born?

That lady whose life has been spent
Worshiping spoken and broken promises;
Called to the carpet, she
Begins to speak, stops, coughs and then…
But what cough is more pleasing?
What youth is more lost?
She toils beneath an unreasoned hatred,
And when assessed, ignores the lover's cost.
Now face to face with the cowboy,
She holds out the rags that once were worn,
As if he were Midas and touched all, would change to
When dust, next to nothing, was born.

In truth two hearts seldom beat as one;
Not without interruptions that we can't pretend to understand.
Some crush it under foot, others under stone;
Some prefer to feel it tremble, as it passes through their hands.
Seasons swim into each other; innocence emerges,
While I contemplate empty cups on table tops.
I get letters from the west coast, advice from friends,
But I'd prefer to wait until they fill these up.
Laughing out loud, strangers turn. I am alone in the laughter.
They misunderstand the comedy of this storm.
Here in the eye of the hurricane, re-witnessing the day
When dust, next to nothing, was born.

The demand for too much and for far too long
Became pointless, absurd and redundant.
The heart and the purse became one,
And they went separate ways in their search for abundance.
I can't even recall her name,
Blameless though, as that changed from day to day.
What name to call her now?
And even if I knew, what is left to say?
Now she beckons to me from across the bar.
Pretending not to notice, I turn,
Hearing the whispers of the lucky and the luckless carried back to
When dust, next to nothing, was born.

An Old Woman's Song

It was just after noon
When the sun hit the dark space,
And the dust swirled in shadows,
As the smile left her face.
She had been blessed with the years
That now she toils under.
She had survived her doubts,
When they roared like the thunder.
Alone in the moment,
She remembers each ghost.
But her memory's a circle
Tied by one loved the most.

She looks in the mirror,
Though that can't hold her attention,
For the refection she sees,
Lies beyond her retention.
Instead her eyes hold a picture,
That moves like wind past her fingers,
And she grasps in frustration,
Until only sadness dares linger.
Now the tears fill the wrinkles,
Where once smiles were the host,
For her memory's a circle
Tied by one loved the most.

As the moon fills her window,
She lays her head on the glass.
She watches and wonders
How it all came to pass.
She's been lonely before,
But she's all alone now.
She feels she could change things
If she only knew how.
So she raises a wine glass,
And offers a toast,
To her memory, a circle,
Tied by one loved the most.

Lines Composed Upon Hearing
of a Lover Who Plans to Wed

When she told me the news, my attention focused in contemplation
On images dancing cloud to cloud,
Apparitions of safety that chained me to sorrow,
In a waste of pride, on the all, too proud.
Would she float to me? Or I to she?
Not in the sadness of yesterday, but with shared affection.
Surely once all is done and said,
Our lives and loves renewed, we must follow our direction.
Bitterness is such a waste, forgotten now,
Dressed in mist, but a blur,
Once again we share a happiness.
I am happy for her.

Yesterday, between sighs, we talked
Beneath the highest sky of spring.
I have done so much in the past few months,
But accomplished nary a thing.
Was it the sun's warmth or forgiveness
That melted those invisible bars,
Freeing the prisoner, killing the lunatic,
Sending lightening upward in search of stars?
In the tenderness of that moment, I kissed her cheek;
One could feel the senses soar,
Eyes no longer weary, but locked in love.
I am happy for her.

I have thrown dirt on the graves of my fathers,
And in the same motion, gone from rags to riches.
But what matters wealth, now or ever?
All the world's money could not open those ditches.
She thought I was reckless, ah well, I suppose …
She said I was generous down to a fault.
I left her a sorrow huge as an immobile stone;
Only time's erosion could shatter that rock.
I think of the fates that brought us together,
And thanking same, in joy concur.
We do not lose sleep over all that is gentle.
I am happy for her.

The End of the Day (Requiem)

The rain falls in buckets.
Lightening flashes and cracks.
The burdens are heavy.
The wind just attacks.
I hear a heart beating
Like the sound of a drum.
I'm so tired of waiting,
But I've got nowhere to run.
Shadows are crawling
Over grass, over clay.
The sunlight is fading.
It's the end of the day.

You can bend but not break it.
You may be sentenced to life.
You can live for tomorrow,
Or just struggle through strife.
Some things are enticing.
Others float like the air.
You have time you can spend,
But none you can spare.

There are folks who keep talking
When they have nothing to say.
The sunlight is fading.
It's the end of the day.

Now my glass sits half empty.
I can't spill a drop.
You better keep moving,
Because one day you will stop.
You need to embrace it,
And forget what's been lost.
You will get other chances,
But they all have a cost.
Look at the mountains
You couldn't move but made sway.
The sunlight has faded,
It's the end of the day.

The Rain, the Night and the Television

The rain, the night, and the television;
Not a drop in my glass left to drink.
Feel like I'm caught in a maze of mirrors,
And there's not a moment to think.
Should I mention the past or ignore the nostalgia?
Pushed by the clock, going blind,
Lately I'm puzzled by all of these women
Who need men, though that's borderline.
Awaiting the morning, preparing for sunrise,
I stare through the grayed windowpane.
Pools of light puddles dancing below me;
The TV, the night and the rain.

The room, the laughs and the old photograph
Now wrinkled, the wrinkles of age.
As I grow older, I'm less likely to wonder.
Like a book, I'm turning the page.
I glance at the infant, and the rush of the memories
Pour through my mind in a flood.
The questions, like darkness, continue to haunt me,
Since I washed my hands of your blood.
Awaiting the sunrise means waiting until morning;
Sitting back, I lose the feeling of doom.
You keep building bridges, so I'm forced to burn them.
The photo, the laughs, and the room.

The dawn, the light, and the television;
What has become of the years?
Once we had forever, but now there's no resting,
Pushed as we are by our fears.
Do you still see me the way that you saw me,
Or are you alone, deep in thought?
Am I the thief still too busy stealing
To notice that he's already been caught?
Awaiting the evening means waiting for twilight,
Urged by the hours moving on,
Awaiting that hour that might bring us together;
The TV, the light, and the dawn.

The Juggler's Song

Deep in the silver shade of twilight,
I can hear the city's chants,
The noise of coughing engines,
And the tones that leave you flat.
Soon the night will form a cover
That sends explosions with each breath.
He sits with his love in one hand,
While the other holds it's death.

Below his unlocked window,
There walks a woman who looks up.
He prays that he is out of sight,
But then his memory interrupts.
There, hard breathing ends in stillness
And surrender of the flesh.
He sits with his love in one hand,
While the other holds it's death.

He can't describe his feelings,
Though it's true he's had some flings.
Something gently gnaws at his heart,
And brings an unexpected sting.
He thought he had the answer,
But it became a game of chess.
He sits with his love in one hand,
While the other holds it's death.

Anthracite

I won't go back to where it started;
That place is a million miles from here.
It's a town that can leave you broken-hearted,
And the weather's never clear.
The houses still sit on that hill,
But the coal's been hauled away.
The piercing wind is never still.
I'll bet its blowing hard today.

You know the bars are always full
Because there's nothing else to do.
That's where you hear them spew the bull,
And we're not talking about a few.
As a boy, I couldn't wait to leave.
When I tried, the car would stall.
Too many lies—too much to grieve—
It's where I watched my father's fall.

There are hearses rolling every day;
When they leave you hear the laughter.
They can't let death get in the way,
Of whatever it is they're after.
It's not hard to find a Dollar Store,
Or an American Legion.
You will wonder what you came here for,
When you visit the Anthracite region.

Wedding Song

The snow was slowly melting,
With the river on the rise.
You were standing open-handed,
With the sun blinding your eyes.
I tend to go against the grain,
And I'd never sell you short.
I learned that lesson years ago,
When I needed your support.
I tend to favor whiskey, and stay away from gin.
I was rolling on in, like the thunder in the wind.

That lady was as good as gold,
And she tasted like fine wine.
The night was dark, the moon cloud-hidden,
When I crossed the line.
The hours passed so slowly,
I had to shake her from her sleep.
That was so many years ago,
When I made that midnight creep.
Listen to the sweet sound of that mandolin;
I was rolling on in, like the thunder in the wind.

The glasses lined up on the table;
There are things you don't forget;

Listening to Wind and Wood,
On the evening that we met.
That evening when I left the club,
I was feeling light as air,
And I was thinking that eventually,
We'd play truth or dare.
Right up until that very day, I was worn thin;
Then I was rolling on in, like the thunder in the wind.

I can't forget that July day;
We were standing in the sun.
I knew that very moment,
That something special had begun.
We started in the Peace Church;
To this day I feel the kiss.
If I didn't admit to being lucky,
Then I'd be remiss.
I remember that the wedding vows sounded like a hymn;
Then we were rolling on in, like the thunder in the wind.

Hell is Empty (The Devil's are All Here)

The fat is in the fire that's leaping like a kite.
A marching band is on the move, and the music sounds bizarre.
There's a fellow ruling Russia,
And he must think that he's a czar.
There are those who put you to the test.
There are those who rule through fear.
Shakespeare said it first and best,
'Hell is empty; the devils are all here.'

They keep searching for an airplane.
The blade-runner is on trial.
Troops are massing near the border,
And the newsmen force their smiles.
Some folks are happy with a job;
While some want a career.
Shakespeare said it first and best,
'Hell is empty, the devils are all here.'

Storms are filled with rain and thunder,
In the night the politician's looting.
Seems like Jesse James is back in Kansas;
There has been another shooting.
Things get very quiet in the courtroom,
Where the judges hide their sneers.
Shakespeare said it first and best,
'Hell is empty, the devils are all here.'

Lightening flashes in the distance.
Folks are talking bombs and taxes.
Some claim that reality TV
Is like a potion that relaxes.
It's really not much different
Than the lions the Romans cheered.
Shakespeare said it first and best,
'Hell is empty, the devils are all here.'

They are finding babies dead in boxes;
Other victims drown in mud.
There are things that can't be covered up,
Unless you wash your hands in blood.
A maniac's hands are on the wheel,
But he's never learned to steer.

Shakespeare said it first and best,
'Hell is empty, the devils are all here.'

The past holds nothing different
Than what's going on today.
Each era has a bag man
Who slips silently away.
In the middle of his last night,
Did JFK know the end was near?
Shakespeare said it first and best,
'Hell is empty, the devils are all here.'

I'm Just Alone (I'm Not Blind)

Well you sure can't be a fantasy,
Though you're dressed up like a dream.
You've been on a shopping spree,
And you think you purchased me.
I feel like an item in a bargain basement,
When you ask to share some time.
I can't help but answer,
'I'm just alone, I'm not blind.'

You say you're one in a million;
I'll need time to check on that.
I just wish that, in the meantime,
You stopped claiming you're where it's at.
You were taking too much credit,
When you said you had half a mind.
I admit I hid my laughter.
I'm just alone, I'm not blind.

Are you always this persistent?
Or is this something new?
We've never even started,
And you don't get it that we're through.
Perhaps I've been too subtle
In my effort to be kind.
Now listen closely. Read my lips.
I'm just alone, I'm not blind.

A Misplaced Generation

I suppose I was drinking at the well for some time;
Strange, how the waters appeared so landscaped.
Getting harder to swallow, as the years flow like sand;
Once grasped with firmness, slow trickle, escape.
Picture him now, much the lord in his castle;
He owns golden pipes. His music's inspired.
Peace at a price and dearly it's cost him,
But, with the slow trickle, he has been reconciled.
In youth it's all different;
You draw the line sharply.
The winters are colder.
The path is like glass.
With age you grow lazy,
Wrapping strings on your fingers.
It's a shame we grow older,
But time has to pass.
You can bathe in breezes summer sent.
You can vote for Hillary Rodham.
You can turn the whole world upside down,
And find the top's much like the bottom.

Birds of a Feather

I'm staring out the window,
Without much on my mind.
The days were getting shorter,
When she left it all behind.
I can sense a storm is coming;
The clouds are low and dark.
I sure don't feel like racing,
But that man said, "on your mark."
There will come a time you realize you lost more than you thought;
Though it's true you can't remember the reason why that war was fought.

This winter's been a cold one
The snows still on the ground.
I've got my ear against the rail
But I don't hear a sound.
It's early in the evening
I can see the sun is setting.
It's when I'm trying to remember
That I do my best forgetting.
It's true I visit cemeteries, I've seen quite a few tombstones,
There are times it makes more sense to leave well enough alone.

There are too many people
Who are left with far too little time,
I see you reaching for the ceiling
While I'm stopping on a dime.
You took the truth and twisted it
Until you made it false,
You knew I couldn't join you
In that little waltz.
It's hard to believe that you and I ever lived together,
I think it's safe to say that we weren't birds of a feather.

Apostle

by
Corrigan Farley

An apostle, he stands,
Swaying to the sound
Of forgotten renown; a legacy
That never should have been.

Alone, the wind runs through him,
Fluttering his cloak, cooling
The face of a man
That never should have been.

Above, afternoon's dying sun.
A solitary vulture soars
Over a sun-scorched land,
That never could have been.

Beneath him: cracked earth, barren
And lifeless. A monument to
The arrogance of man, to a world
That never should have been.

A rope caresses his neck.
From side to side,
He swings.

Night Plight (Bitterness Passing)

Is that destiny's howl, or just the wind's wild approach?
The strongest trees quiver and shake.
Of the voices below, there are none that I know,
But they all tend to dwell on mistakes.
I hear the songs of the street,
At once cold and complete,
And the singer's a slave to his task.
She wore emeralds and mink,
And often stood on the brink,
Before stepping from behind her mask.
I don't want to complain
About being washed by the rain,
Nor dwell on the cause of the flight.
But as the sun pulls its stakes,
The darkness awakes,
And with it, I'm joined by night plight.

The candlelight flickers; the flame dies; I curse,
As I'm pierced by midnight's bayonet.
The warrior is busy; thought makes me dizzy;
It's tangled and smells of cement.
One thing is certain,
As I pull back the curtain,
The target of all of my taunts.
It was never my habit,
To risk it all on a gambit,
And that is the spirit that haunts.
My vision, my memory,
The way that it came to me;
This evening that holds me so tight.
Makes no sense to recall
The way it all stalled,
And got stuck in the shape of night plight.

No knock on the door, as the cold truth invades;
Like always, she throws loaded dice.
I stand on the trapdoor, a bluff nothing more;
Still sometimes a dodge will suffice.
I'm not speaking of need;
Perhaps want; maybe greed.
If there's a difference, it's one I can't find.
I'm not that upset,

But remorse and regret
Found a home on the outskirts of mind.
The philanderer grins;
As the clock starts to spin,
I confess I don't share his delight.
Is this feeling grotesque?
Or, am I simply obsessed
By this product of another night plight?

There is light in the distance, as daylight approaches.
You'll see me and learn I survived.
If this sounds at all bitter, it's the flowers that wither,
And that moment has finally arrived.
My vision is failing;
The sun hits my railing;
I conquer the source of my gloom.
The darkness is reeling; there is light on the ceiling,
And it spreads to the ends of the room.
You begged, lied and pleaded,
Which just wasn't needed.
Did we make it? Be honest, not quite.
We simply buried the treasure.
I rejected your pleasure;
Chose instead to combat my night plight.

She found me there, shattered on top of the rocks,
As she danced her way into a dream.
She whispered 'she loved me' and I, thinking of me,
Said 'it's best we avoid those extremes.'
But that argument's witless,
As I for one witnessed,
When she held out the wine in her hands.
And while we were drinking,
She said, 'I've been thinking,
It's time you told me where you stand.'
You pay for each blunder,
With headaches like thunder.
She winked when I spoke of my gripes.
And closing the door,
She said 'say no more'
As she ushered away my night plight.

Twins

I was dreaming of voices blown like horns;
The capture of sound within a sound born.
And that birth implored me, listen,
And then it begged to warn,
And finally simply to pretend.
In the manner of children that future touch,
And then in wonder ... wander much
Into tunnels without end.

The dream led onto dream, until
The scent of one lone daffodil
Was picked up by the breeze and carried,
And to some other scent was married.
Yet, it's scent still stood apart.
Like I recalling other days,
With the wings of butterflies,
Could only pray the moment be raised,
And held somewhere inside my heart.

Still we'll not regret these or those days.
It matters not the month or hour.
It's all found in the ways,
Their tongues can soothe; their features flatter;

Their smiles rebuild what time would shatter.
They are in flight;
I've watched the shadows
Beneath green on blue and blue on green.
And all else there that could be seen,
Grew small, lost in their glow.

Judas Kiss

Deny it, you have to, but you were the liar,
Each and every time you moved your mouth.
But you sold your soul to the devil when you took that flier,
Only you have more than that in common with Faust.
Reach for the star you once held in your fist;
A planet way out of reach now.
Have you ever learned to perfect that Judas kiss?

An Afternoon at Gullifty's
(The Price is Right)

I swear this place is haunted,
But I'm not afraid of ghosts.
They can sit right here beside me,
And I'd be a gracious host.
I met two women within these walls;
One grew full with spite.
The other cut the darkness;
She seemed to move with candlelight.

I lost my soul a floor below.
It took me years to get it back.
Now my feet don't ever touch those stairs;
I didn't know the deck was stacked.
Outside a flag blows in the wind;
Some birds take to the skies.
I met the other woman through that door,
Back when my hopes began to rise.

Drew Carey's on the television;
There's a jukebox on my left.
That lady deserved to go to jail;
I considered it grand theft.
A school bus is passing by
A shop called the Crimson Frog,

There's a woman in the parking lot
Out to walk her dog.

The bartender is mixing drinks;
The waitress wears a frown.
There's a customer a few stools down
Working on getting his sorrows drowned.
I can still recall the day we met,
When I took things to extremes.
Someone just wished me the best of luck;
I have no idea what he means.

I'm staring out the window,
But now I can't see a thing.
Won't let my mind slip back in time;
I know the trouble that could bring.
There's a reflection in the mirror,
But I don't recognize the face.
I wonder where that young man went;
He left in too much haste.

The tables all sit empty;
There are flowers on the fence.
Thoughts are flowing through my brain,
And they are in the present tense.
There are bottles lined up on the shelf,
But I won't touch a drop,
A song keeps playing in my head,
And I wish that it would stop.

I heard she settled out near Pittsburgh,
Where she lost her tractor man.
I guess that's just the way things go,
When lies begin your plans.
I still wake up with the woman
That I've loved for more than thirty years.
Somebody just played a Dylan tune;
He wants that bottle over here.

The Mindful Eye

Was the nature of a dream our meeting,
Surreal, passionately dark and fleeting;
Lacking beginnings, untouched by ends,
Filled with images of curves and bends?
There you stood, eclipsing beauty,
Breaking waves beneath stars shooting.
Mist was rising from the water;
The woman rising from the daughter.
And now those distant shapes we kiss;
In letters wonder what was missed.
I, the eye that scanned the thigh,
While you insist the mindful eye.

Sadly the Sterile Scorpion
(Ode to the Queen of Spades)

This fever's independent of temperature,
Infecting every image with decay.
Seems like heat is apt to follow you anywhere,
While warmth just moves further away.
There's a dangerous distance involved in this,
Like the strain of confronting a mirror.
You keep moving closer until you stand face to face,
But nothing ever gets clearer.
A storyteller memorized one side of things
Using words that have changed through the years,
Spun by a borderline junkie with an alcohol crutch
That hangs just atop of her fears.
A voice, it appears, a thin mist on the glass;
Stained music the image of breath.
Love may be the product when one's taught how to live,
But all that is life ebbs to death.

On a social ladder with false idol rungs,
One must worship the worst on the climb.
You may recall trading a kiss for a place on the throne,
And a chance to taste the fruit from the vine.
Amazing all the lies born in a sweet desert voice
That abandoned all forms of restraint.
She was cautioned early, but she turned a deaf ear,
And continued to mouth her complaints.
The shadows, a home for the horrors of age;
They wait eager to haunt our recall.
The day will come, you'll reach the highest rung,
Where the choices are step down or fall.
You spent your time slipping both in and out;
You were an artist at molding each breath.
Love may be a product when one's taught how to live,
But all that is life ebbs to death.

Clowns she has challenged, with a depth of disguise;
Deception her art of pursuit.
Well, she swore when we met, she was the Queen of hearts,
Who could tell she'd be changing her suit.
One could hide and ignore the failed masquerade,
The purpose was there—postcard clear.
Imagine the surprise, to climb in that hole,
And discover she'd been insincere.

41

Forever the cynic, this could never work out;
The days overflowed with despair.
A slave to her weakness, she would lose every bout,
And it left her beyond repair.
I built up the courage to let the truth fly,
And she spit on the cross of my breath.
Love may be a product when one's taught how to live,
But all that is life ebbs to death.

Your Frozen Portrait

I can hear the ticking of the clocks;
Time hangs like a chain on me.
Nonsense to heave roseate rocks
Into a long dead sea.
I am standing near the silver shore,
Feeling empty at the core,
But one thing I am looking for:
The sight that bids the searching stall;
Your frozen portrait on the wall.

Below this room, the day takes shape;
Streets, with signs, merge into one.
The heart explodes; the words escape
And drip like honey off the tongue.
Reflections on an opened lid,
Bring to mind emotions that we hid.
I can still sense those things we did,
Yet there's but one scene that I hear call:
Your frozen portrait on the wall.

Of all the gems I left behind,
Near the fountain of my youth,
The depth of loss eats at my soul
And forms the puzzle of my truth.
I watch the country highway twist,
Until it's covered by the mist.
Seems strange that of my memory's list,
There's but one face I can recall:
Your frozen portrait on the wall.

Was on a road of strain and doubt,
Where all the judges have gone blind.
Now and then in wonder ask,
Do I ever cross your mind?
Perhaps its fate or destiny,
To wait for an eternity,
With these eyes that only see,
The shattered frame high in the hall:
Your frozen portrait on the wall.

Song to Annie

These days are haunted by the darkness,
And I can't turn to face the sun.
There are times I hear her singing,
But I know that song's been sung.
Music lived within her,
So when she played it called by name.
To those of us who knew her well,
It will never sound the same.

The last time that I saw her,
She hid the pain behind her eyes.
So I didn't know how much it meant,
When we said our goodbyes.
Today I sit in pieces,
Cursing life that's so unfair;
Would give a woman of her worth
A weight she could not bear.

Sometimes I think of her with laughter;
At times my thought is full with tears.
I see her in both Wind and Wood,
And probably will for all my years.
But for now I chase a shadow,
Of what was here before;
For the shadows all that's left to me,
As the limo waits no more.

The View From Oblivion's Corner

Crawling through the night, spilling and refilling cups of wine;
Ripped by love and hatred and finding any difference borderline.
Your guards deceit and anger have been posted at your gates;
They cast reflections on the water this is the stuff the dark creates.
You always feared the gypsy would return as though a queen,
But I was never into royal blood; it stains in blues and greens.
And you ought to know my feelings on rings and jewels and kings.
It all seems so moronic these titles birth can bring.
Once you cut the tightrope on me; you recall that's how we met.
I landed right on top of you, as you were taking down the net.
You told me that you loved me, but you left me on the floor.
It's gotten so it's hard to tell your windows from your doors.
The drunkard at the river's edge duels a maze of misconception;
I guess he never found a bargain when he bartered for affection.
There's a note inside a bottle, but it breaks not far from shore.
Your sailor sweeps the waters clean, while the drunkard drinks some more.
It's a melancholy subject; these feelings, this desire.
Why water down the present with the antiques still on fire?
Standing on your balcony, you toss notes toward the street.
I'd suggest you use a pigeon, but you never were discreet.
Beauty bends to future's judgment and, without depth, it dies.
There's a trace of pure amphetamine still alive inside your eyes.
The drunkard keeps a tombstone, where he carves this epitaph:
'Your love was more like larceny—petty in it's wrath.'

The Degradation Inn

These many years, I often traveled incognito
With a calumet my one and only friend.
Now, I question as to why the myth exploded;
Seems the Dies Irae is drawing to an end.
Who limps quietly into the great division?
A minstrel there, at his side a mandolin,
As darkness fell and obscured the castle,
When they told me there was no room at the inn.

Sold my life preserver to a band of gypsies
Who harmonized beneath the mackerel skies.
Found Narcissus with his head bowed in reflection,
And no signs of regret inside his eyes.
The scowling blind assassin bought his entrance;
Secret phantom there was no denying him.
When I arrived I found he had left a message;
It read that there was no room at the inn.

A banker screamed and joined in the Fandango,
While Beau Brummell was searching for his voice.
I heard he lost it in a barroom playing Pope Joan;
When you gamble you are left a Hobson's choice.
All the kingfish stood holding out promotions
To Pegasus for erasing crimes worn thin.
Janus slept as the saboteur slipped past him,
Only to find that there was no room at the inn.

Called Camelot, a prince sounded a warning.
Two pink flamingos floundered in the sand;
They sang Bhagavad-Gita with an angel's chorus
While Lorelei, laughing, clapped her hands.
The Juggernaut of fate renounced the devil,
Once the rug was pulled exposing all his sins.
And Beelzebub was left philosophizing
About the need for more rooms at the inn.

I rode with Charon but found him un-amusing,
Once he declared the flood an act of god.
Plus his sale of morello's to the masses,
While he picked their teeth with a lightening rod.
The Flying Dutchman lies low beneath the surface;
The ships have all but ceased their coming in.

And Proteus owns the only face that's smiling,
As he tells me there are no rooms at the inn.

It's true that, when telling stories, words suffice,
For little else slips through____
In waking, find related dreams
That colored my night's view.
In time it's time to speak of these
Without the strength of gin.
For every good and evil lurks
At the degradation inn.

The Stubborn Memory Blues

I'm outside in air so heavy,
You have to carry it when you walk.
It brings to mind that summer,
Years ago, when we still talked.
Now I'm no longer weary;
I can sleep. I'm not upset.
I'm not saying that I remember;
It's more like I can't forget.

We had wine that day in Jersey.
We had cheese in Delaware.
When you told me you were leaving,
I think I said I didn't care.
You know that's not the last time,
That I laid down a losing bet.
I'm not saying that I remember;
It's more like I can't forget.

I know a woman who tells me stories;
She likes to sneak up from behind.
I swear that she gets pleasure,
As she bends and twists my mind.
Now I don't have a dark side;
I think I lost that when we met.
I'm not saying that I remember;
It's more like I can't forget.

The evening sky is scarred by lightening,
And the rain pounds on the glass.
I pour myself an Irish whiskey,
And I let these feelings pass.
That giant oaks still standing,
With leaves that seem to sweat.
I'm not saying that I remember;
It's more like I can't forget.

The last time that I saw her,
The new century had just begun.
So I didn't see it coming,
When she said she had to run.
My plane ride home was bumpy,
And it hasn't touched down yet.

I'm not saying that I remember;
It's more like I can't forget.

I had a woman in Alabama,
And another in Tennessee.
The one liked riding horses;
The other liked riding me.
So I seldom hit the deep south,
And I don't have one regret.
I'm not saying that I remember;
It's more like I can't forget.

The lazy rivers crawling,
And the eagle's on the climb.
The old barn door is closing,
And the fruit rots on the vine.
Sometimes trying to please a woman
Can be like fishing without a net.
I'm not saying that I remember;
It's more like I can't forget.

A Sign of the Times

The evening fell, a fog through lamplight.
His breath was hanging in the air.
She was standing on the corner, stranded,
With the wind in her hair.
In the mist, she thought she sensed a figure;
Too much Hitchcock in her younger years.
But, in a motion, he was there beside her,
Whispering in her ears.
She had eyes like the stars and hair the color of Mars;
The words she spoke were dressed in rhymes.
She told him, then, her independence
Was just a sign of the times.

He sat rehearsing lines atop a barstool,
Nursing down another beer.
She noticed that his hands were shaking,
As he drew her near.
The music seemed to float around her;
She touched his hand which led to dance.
Her every move was fueled by passion,
And so he took a chance.
Her affairs were so brief that he felt like a thief
Who cannot face up to his crimes.
But, in his heart, he knew the guilt
Was just a sign of the times.

It was dawn when he reached out to touch her,
But she had vanished in the dark.
He threw away the note she left him,
Leaving unread remarks.
He tried to cry but felt no sorrow,
As he bathed in the morning light,
Contemplating how to waste his time
Until the day turned to night.
When the hunt begins with lies and assorted sins
Committed over drinks served with limes,
Nobody even asks for a reason;
It's just a sign of the times.

Lines Composed in the Foyer
(The Flight of Eros)

In this twilight contemplation;
In the damp darkness of despair,
Where fate looms like a mountain,
And tears hang in the air;
Through memories maze, an empty hourglass
Bends the slaves of time,
Into the shapes of innocence
And their shadows into rhyme.
I watch the waves retreating
To be renewed for the assault;
They sweep away the stones of shame
And drown the weeds of fault.
The echo of their thunder
Fades just beyond my grasp,
As it rumbles like a wheel of fire
That cuts the truth in half.

All the friendships born in autumn;
All the high hopes of the spring;
In dreams transformed from lambs to lions,
Now they eat through everything.
In the narrow pass of honesty,
Embarrassment lies dead,
Near the broken blade of anger's sword,
And those words that should not have been said.
I can hear the raging voices
Still to whispers in the wind,
That blows in circles round my head;
Stops ... then starts again.
In the sadness of these moments,
I strain to see a face,
As I hear the sound of laughter
Beneath a veil of Irish lace.

On the path of lost affection,
One must keep the burdens light;
You may travel on that road for years,
Before sorrow takes to flight.
Beneath the amber skies of ridicule,
In the palm of hatred's hand,
On the swollen tongue of jealousy,
Where nothing straight can stand.

I still feel the fires within me
In forms of tension un-subdued,
And when life seems the harshest,
I am soothed by time spent with you.
There are explosions in all happiness,
Mixed feelings and borderlines.
Love is the prism of the inevitable,
Lost on the battleground of the mind.

A Fool's Heart (Part 2)

He still can't remember where he was,
Though he'd been there before.
The waves were licking at his feet,
As he walked along the shore.
She moved as though a melody,
And he felt a sonnet start.
The sun was sinking in the sea;
She in the fool's heart.

He took some sand into his hand;
Grains trickled through his grasp.
She said, 'I've seen your face before—
It's like an echo from my past.'
She didn't look familiar,
But he vowed to do his part.
The waves were fast retreating
Quite unlike the fool's heart.

He told her he'd been crucified,
And was forced to sleep on nails;
That he even knew a woman,
Who once threatened him with jail.
He was hungrier than a refugee,
Whose world's been blown apart;
A comic trapped by tragedy,
That had broke the fool's heart.

The twilight dimmed to owl-light.
The moon grew full and pink.
They sat together in a bar,
Where she paid for the drinks.
A chain of gold hung round her neck;
Her eyes were soft and dark,
And as he was falling into them,
She caught the fool's heart.

They played, she won, a game of pool.
Then she gave the table up.
She leaned upon his every word,
And never sought to interrupt.
She told him there's no answers,
But that questioning's an art

He knew that she had slipped inside,
And touched the fool's heart.

At dawn, they woke up on the beach.
He held her in his arms.
He sensed that if he let her go,
Would only do him harm.
That very day they rode away;
The horse before the cart.
He felt the twist of sorrow lift.
She had healed the fool's heart.

Traveling the Commonwealth

There's sunlight on the river.
A boat sits near the shore.
That man looks so forsaken,
He sure can't take much more.
You say that you've seen everything,
But then you opened up your eyes.
It was then that you were blinded,
By the weight of all those lies.
I spent some time in Pittsburgh.
I've been to Station Square.
I sailed down that river.
Right now I'm just not there.

The sky is dark and cloudy;
The rain forms puddles on the ground.
She was leaning on some poetry.
She was reading Ezra Pound.
It's true I spent some mornings,
Underneath a golden dome.
Her feet have touched the pavements,
That rest above the catacombs.
There's much history in Philly.
You may go by it way too fast.
She changes like the weather,
And it can't be forecast.

The winter sky is pale,
And the criminal is shady.
Sometimes it takes more than a lifetime,
To get close to a lady.
She took a trip to Baltimore,
And never once apologized.
When she returned to Harrisburg,
She was the one who criticized.
I've spent some time in Scranton,
Before I crossed that off my list.
There are times you get an offer,
That's simply too hard to resist.

Sometimes dreams can turn so murky,
That they muddle up the mind.
I spent a day on Mulberry Street
With a woman I can't find.

I feel like going to the movies;
I've already taken in a few.
That day passed by so quickly,
At a pace you only knew.
If you ever get to Erie,
You can see the pot of death.
I ran away from Hazleton
And it left me short of breath.

The Moon Pass Through The Glass

It was an acid colored autumn,
We spent polishing our fears.
I would burlesque like a jester,
As was the style in all those years.
With great care, we took precautions,
Always speaking tongue in cheek;
And we swallowed our objections,
But that only left us weak.
So when we found it over,
You escaped beyond the din.
I stood face to face with Pluto,
As the room began to spin.
A fire, a furnace, the ever present blast,
As I watched the moon pass through the glass.

To my eyes each sight was classic,
Not a still-life blur to steal.
But, I was always the romantic,
While your paintings were surreal.
I remember all the anger,
As more than flesh and bone could bear.
And it was never in our natures,
To act with grace while so aware.
When the music stained your window,
There was little left to say.

No, I never hated anyone.
It just took too much to stay.
It seemed to me my blood was flowing fast,
As I watched the moon pass through the glass.

Now this buffoon speaks much softer
Than the insane roar you heard.
But in matters of this measure,
I still use all the same words.
And you're not ever noiseless;
Just today your sister came.
She stood before me, death-like,
And screamed out, 'you're to blame.'
You point to all my blossoms,
And you claim I let them wilt.
While I'll not accept your censure,
I will bear my share of guilt.
It seemed to me each breath would be my last,
As I watched the moon pass through the glass.

Graduation

by
Corrigan Farley

Step over the crumpled remains of self,
But never let futures lie.
Live above all bounds,
Yet follow the eastern sky.

Turn towards a radiant glow
Of ecstasy oft-denied.
Race life's fading lines;
And forsake midnight's cry.

Walk affront of abandoned dreams,
Carving one's own way.
Let nothing stay your path,
Yet keep yourself at bay.

Now step past the border of dawn,
And paw through the last shroud of grey.
As you stand on the threshold of a different tomorrow
Rise up and greet the new day.

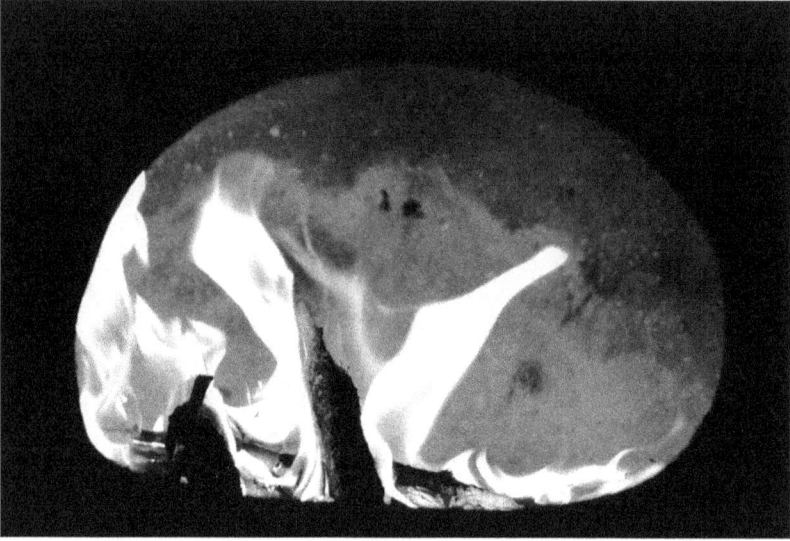

Burning Ash (Sharon's Song)

I wonder on this warmth: is it the fire, the whiskey, or the woman?
She laughs, rolls her eyes, and calls my bluff.
Outside, the rain raps hard against the window.
She pulls me close and says, 'you've had enough.'
These little jokes are really invitations,
Though it's when we kiss the bottle disappears.
Then teasingly she says, 'I want you sober.'
While, playfully, I pretend that I don't hear.
Lying back, her hair falls smooth against silk pillows,
Where the shadows dance a waltz across her face.
It is then I feel the tug of my emotions,
As the outline of her form my fingers trace.
An hour later, still awake, burning ash where there was fire,
I love to love and I love the memory too.
And it comes to me in waves the warmth is feeling,
Not felt for years until I made love with you.